THE BEST OF
"BRAKES"

AN ACTIVITY BOOK
FOR KIDS WITH
ADD

Published by
MAGINATION PRESS
An Educational Publishing Foundation Book
American Psychological Association
750 First Street, NE
Washington, DC 20002

For more information about our books, including a complete catalog,
please write to us, call 1-800-374-2721, or visit our website at www.maginationpress.com

Library of Congress Cataloging-in-Publication Data

The best of "Brakes" : an activity book for kids with ADD / [edited by] Patricia O. Quinn
and Judith M. Stern ; illustrated by Kate Sternberg.
        p.   cm.
Summary: A collection of articles, games, puzzles, activities, suggestions,
and resources, which were previously published in the newsletter "Brakes,"
for children with attention deficit disorder.
ISBN 1-55798-661-4 (pbk.)
1. Attention-deficit-disordered children—Education (Elementary)—Juvenile literature.
2. Attention-deficit-disordered children—Recreation—Juvenile literature.
3. Hyperactive children—Education (Elementary)—Juvenile literature.
4. Hyperactive children—Recreation—Juvenile literature.
5. Creative activities and seat work—Juvenile literature.
[1. Attention-deficit hyperactivity disorder.] I. Title: Activity book for kids with ADD.
II. Quinn, Patricia O. III. Stern, Judith M. IV. Sternberg, Kate, 1954-, ill.

LC4713.2 .B48 2000
371.93—dc21   99-057770

Manufactured in the United States of America
10 9 8 7 6 5 4 3 2 1

THE BEST OF
"BRAKES"

AN ACTIVITY BOOK
FOR KIDS WITH
ADD

edited by
Patricia O. Quinn, M.D., and Judith M. Stern, M.A.

with illustrations by
Kate Sternberg

MAGINATION PRESS • WASHINGTON, DC

TABLE OF CONTENTS

PART 2: HAVING FUN! RECREATION & SPORTS..33

PART 3: MAKING AND KEEPING FRIENDS. . .53

PART 4: LOOKING AT FEELINGS. . .61

PART 5: YOUR FAMILY AND YOU. . .71

INTRODUCTION

*W*elcome to *The Best of BRAKES*, an activity book written especially for kids with attention deficit disorder, with or without hyperactivity. Published by Magination Press from 1994 to 1998, *BRAKES* was a newsletter that helped boys and girls between ages 8 and 13 learn more about themselves and their ADD. It also helped them feel connected to other kids who were dealing with similar issues. With information-packed feature articles, games, puzzles, and letters, *BRAKES* offered helpful suggestions and solutions to everyday problems involving homework, getting along with others, and becoming better organized. Kids as well as teachers, counselors, and other professionals shared their great ideas. And the collection was all too good to keep to ourselves.

The Best of BRAKES contains an assortment of our favorite articles and activities, presented in five subject areas: school, sports and recreation, friends, feelings, and family. You can enjoy these pages in any order you choose. If you are working with a counselor or in a group, you might like to complete some of these activities together. No matter how you use this activity book, you will learn a lot about yourself and about how to make the most of your many talents and abilities — while having fun!

For readers who have seen *BRAKES* in the past, here is an opportunity to catch up on activities you may have missed or were too young to appreciate. For kids who are not familiar with *BRAKES*, you have a treat in store for you. We hope you will find new ideas and helpful hints to make life go more smoothly. Learning about ADD can be fun!

PATRICIA QUINN, M.D.
JUDITH STERN, M.A.

INCREASING SCHOOL SUCCESS

Kids with ADD are just as smart as everyone else. You may have to work a little harder in school when attention problems get in the way, but you are capable of getting good grades and being an excellent student. As you look through this section of the activity book, you may come across some new ideas for getting organized, managing homework, and being a better student. Some of the activities may help you come up with your own ideas for making school life easier.

SECRETS FOR SCHOOL SUCCESS

By Linda Wheelhouse

The following ideas and suggestions could make a real difference in your study and time management skills. Choose some that you think will work for you and make them part of your plan for success.

DEVELOPING GOALS AND STRATEGIES

- Be honest. Identify the obstacles that sometimes get in your way when you do homework or when you have to study.
- Set goals to work on the obstacles that you identify. Make these goals specific and clear so that you will be able to judge if they are successful. For example, "I want to be a better speller" doesn't say how you will accomplish that. Instead say, "I will study weekly for my spelling test."
- Be creative and choose strategies that fit your personality needs. If you are a person who needs to be active, try studying while pedaling a stationary bicycle. If you like to be around people, try studying with a friend.
- Set up a regular time and special place to study.
- If you tend to forget your books, see if you can get an extra set for use at home.

PRIORITIZE ACTIVITIES

- Remember, you can't do everything in one day. Decide what is most important to accomplish each day. Be realistic about how much time you have. Using a schedule or planner sometimes helps you organize your time. It may help you to determine what is important by talking things over with an adult. Your teacher, tutor, or parents might be able to help you out here.
- Like many people, you may find it hard to study when you would rather be visiting with your friends. When this happens, promise yourself a chance to visit your friend after you have studied for a definite length of time. By offering yourself such a reward you will be more motivated to finish what you need to do.
- Each day look at all your assignments and decide what you need you do 1st, 2nd, 3rd,

etc. Take a red pen and write a number beside each one. Remember, reading and studying are part of homework. Also, don't leave the most difficult assignment for when you are tired.
- Plan to take study breaks. Set a goal for the length of time you will study and then also plan what you will do during the break. For example, write down, "Study for 30 minutes, then take a 5-minute break to eat an apple. I will then study for 20 minutes more."

TIME MANAGEMENT SKILLS

The basis for good study skills is time management. Time management specialists recommend two techniques to consider. "Chunking" and "clustering" are the basics for managing your time. Would you eat a big steak in one bite? Impossible — you might choke. Instead, you would cut it up, which means you would "chunk" it. Should you do a big project in one night? Maybe, but think about the steak. Remember, you don't want to "choke" on your assignment either. Cut the project down into chunks when it is first assigned. Once you can do this, you will be less stressed and might even enjoy doing your project.

Have you figured out yet what "clustering" is? Well, would you eat one piece of rice at a time? You would be at the table all night. Would you go to the library and pick up one book for one class and go back in two days and pick up two more books? You might do that but what a waste of time! You could have spent some time with a best friend instead.

Remember your time is precious. Guard it wisely!

Ms. Wheelhouse is a resource teacher at Ridge School in Rockville, Maryland. She is also a study/time management consultant.

WHAT ARE THE SECRET WORDS?

Color in the shapes with the dots to find the secret to success in school.
You may need to hold the page at an angle to read the answer when finished.

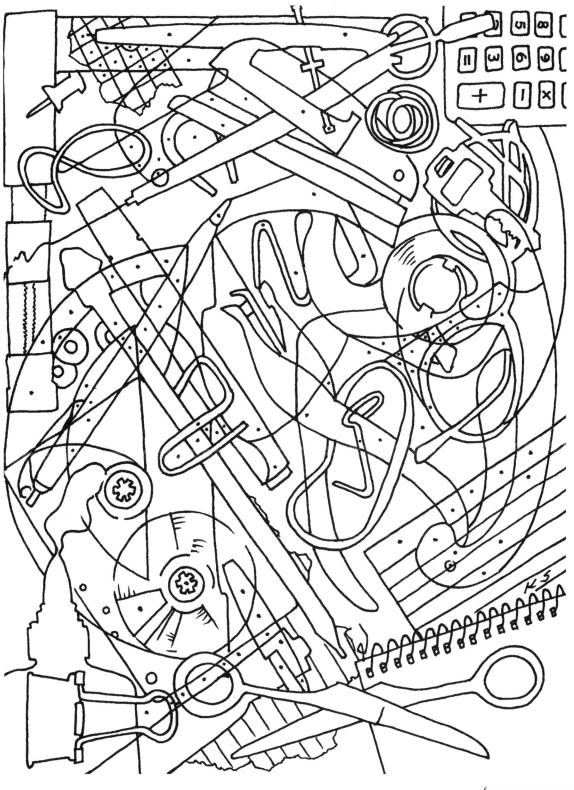

(answer on page 90)

KEEPING ON TRACK

Some kids with ADD have lots of extra energy. This makes it difficult for them to stay in their seats and pay attention during the long school day. Here is some advice from middle school students who shared what worked for them.

- Get in some physical activity each day to work off your energy.

- When you feel like you can't sit another minute, ask the teacher if you can take a "time-out." Discuss this situation with your teacher and make a plan for what you will do during these time-outs.

- Talk to your parents and doctor if you take medication for your hyperactivity and you feel it is not working.

- Make sure to get enough sleep each night and eat a good breakfast.

- Eat a nutritious diet. Cut down on junk food and sweets.

- Ask the teacher if you can sit in the front of the room if this helps you.

- Ask permission to doodle if this helps focus your attention so you can sit longer.

GETTING BETTER ORGANIZED

Before Amy goes to school, she makes a list of everything she will need.
Is there anything on Amy's list that is not in the picture? Is there anything in the picture that is not on Amy's list? Look at Amy carefully. What did she forget to do?

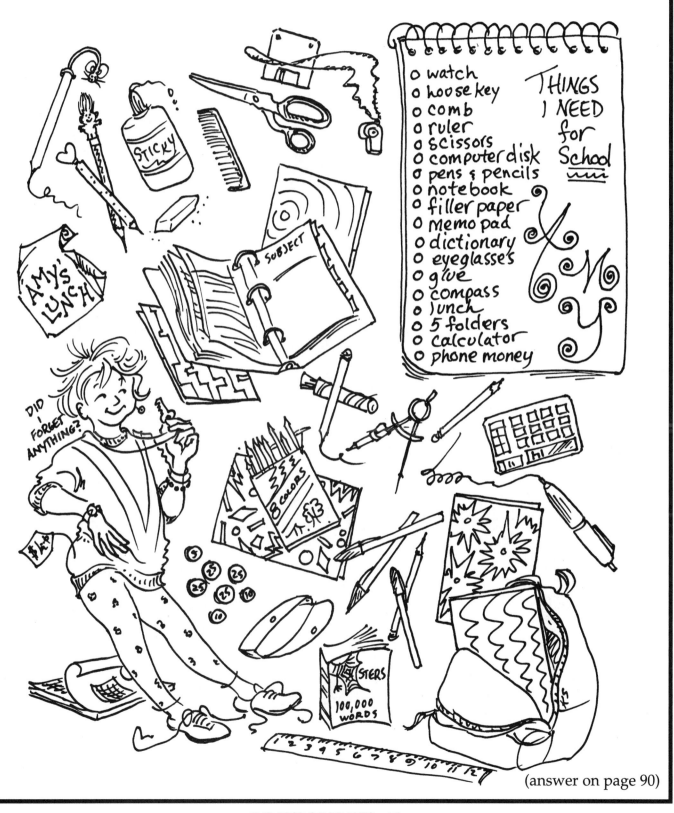

(answer on page 90)

SCHOOL DAYS MAZE

**It is Tom's first day at school.
Help him follow his schedule by passing through
each apple once in the correct order.**

Tom's Schedule

1 Science
2 Math
3 Chorus
4 Lunch
5 Art
6 Social Studies
7 P.E.
8 Language Arts

How to Organize Your Notebook

Kids with ADD need to put extra effort into keeping their notebooks neat. We have found that a three-ring binder works the best. Here is how you can set it up:

- Get enough dividers so that you can make one up for each subject. Then label each divider with one of your school subjects.

- Some students divide each subject in their notebook into half. Use the front half of each section for classwork ONLY. Use the back half for homework assignments for that subject ONLY.

- Keep a "portable" hole puncher in your notebook. Make sure to punch all of your papers that don't have holes. Put them immediately into their correct section. (Ouch! Get that social studies test out of the math section!)

- Don't use the front clip in the notebook to hold work papers. Those papers belong in the subject sections. Use the front only for items that need to go home (such as school notices). Make it a habit to take these important papers out every afternoon before you begin your homework.

- Once your notebook starts to get too thick, put it on a diet. Take out papers you don't need anymore. Ask your teacher(s) if you need help in figuring out what you should keep, what you can leave at home, and what you can throw out.

- It's a good idea to set aside the same day each week to do a notebook "TUNE-UP."

LISTS CAN HELP

Learn to become a "list maker." Start by making a list of all the school supplies you will need, then check off each item as you get it.

Get in the habit of making a list each day after school. Write down all the things that you need to do. Try making this kind of a list:

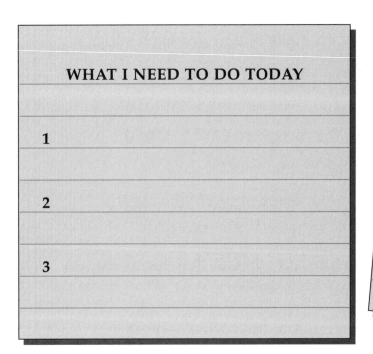

Once you have made your list, give each assignment or activity a number (in order of importance). Keep the list in a place where you can look at it often.

Debbie Ciment
San Antonio, Texas

ARE YOU READY FOR SCHOOL?

Locate these objects that you will need for school:

GLUE BOTTLE	SOCK	LOCK
TEACHER (bearded)	KNAPSACK	PENCIL
SCISSORS	CALCULATOR	RULER
FILLER PAPER	BANANA	KEY
JUICE BOX	SNEAKER	COMPASS
APPLE	COMB	GLASSES
	SANDWICH	

HOW TO IMPROVE YOUR READING SKILLS

Much of what you learn in school comes from the pages of a book. Some kids find it frustrating to be told to read and summarize or to read and answer questions when they are not even sure of what they read or what it meant. Because everyone reads differently, here are some quick and easy ideas to help you better understand what you are reading.

BEFORE YOU BEGIN TO READ

- Look at the title and pictures. Think about what you already know about the topic or story you are getting ready to read. Make predictions about the story or material before you begin to read.

- If there are questions you need to answer about the reading, look them over before you begin. This will help you stay focused and also will help you read for meaning.

- Make sure you look at chapter titles, headings, and subheadings. Paying attention to these will help you find answers to the questions.

WHILE YOU ARE READING

- Stop and ask yourself questions about what you are reading and try to answer them. Keep predicting what will happen next. Check your predictions, change them when necessary, and make new ones as you read on.

- If something you read doesn't make sense, reread it and think about what the words really mean. If it still doesn't make sense, ask someone to read it with you.

- As you read, think about how the information you are reading is like something you already know. Try to make connections.

- When you come to an unfamiliar word, try to figure out what it might mean. Use the words around it or read on and use the rest of the paragraph to figure out what would make sense. If you can't figure it out, ask someone or look up the word in a dictionary.

- Stop occasionally to check your understanding. Retell the part of the story you've just read. If you can't retell it, reread it.

- Make pictures in your mind of what you are reading. Try to visualize the settings, characters, and order of events.

WHEN YOU HAVE FINISHED READING

- Ask yourself what you have learned. Write down some key words to help you remember.

- Summarize the important information in writing, or out loud to a parent or friend, or into a tape recorder.

- Again, try to make connections to what you already know about the subject.

- Answer those questions you were supposed to find out about as you read.

I am sure that you will find it is a lot easier to read for meaning if you have a plan before, during, and after you read. Happy reading!

This article was contributed by Ms. Paula Y. Arons, who is a reading specialist from Cincinnati, OH.

READING IS EVERYWHERE!

How many things can you find to read in this picture?

SOLUTIONS FOR COMMON SCHOOL PROBLEMS IF YOU ARE IN MIDDLE SCHOOL

When you have a problem in school, remember that you don't need to take care of everything alone. Help is always available. Here are some ideas for you to consider.

BECOME YOUR OWN ADVOCATE AT SCHOOL

That means speak up for yourself. You know what works best for you, so you should let your teacher or your counselor know. Talk to your teachers after school and explain your problems to them. If, for example, you have trouble spelling, then suggest that your teacher not count spelling (unless it is your English class!) as part of your grade. Most teachers are very pleased when you take the time to talk to them because then they know that you are trying.

Practice with your parents how you will ask a teacher for help. Don't wait until you feel that you are drowning before asking your teachers for help. It's best to ask in advance so you can avoid problems. You may want to think about what worked well for you last year and make a list of what you and the school can do together.

BE REALISTIC ABOUT WHAT YOU ARE DOING

Don't try to take subjects that may be too much for you at first, such as foreign languages. Listen to your counselor and teachers and follow their course suggestions — even if it means not doing what all of your classmates are doing.

Try not to be a perfectionist. Don't expect too much from yourself at first. When things don't go well, don't stop trying. Others may see giving up as a serious problem because they may think that you don't care about how well you can do. Being honest and being willing to talk about your strengths and weaknesses can make a big difference.

USE AVAILABLE TECHNOLOGY

You are lucky to be born in a generation with computers and other devices that can help. Learn the keyboard so that you can use this technology for all of your classes and for your homework. It could very well be the extra boost that keeps you on top of the workload. Some kids use laptop computers in the classroom so that they can take notes easily.

MAKE FRIENDS WITH A CLASSMATE WHO IS ORGANIZED

Besides having fun together with your classmate, he or she can teach you good organizational skills. Get some of your other classmates' telephone numbers in case you miss a homework assignment.

BELIEVE IN YOURSELF!

Look for solutions to problems. Remember your ADD is an explanation, not an excuse. Help is always available for those who are willing to also helper themselves. Most of all, keep a positive attitude. Believe in yourself. Even if you have to work hard, doing well in school is worth it!

This article is by Linda Halperin, a school psychologist in Livingston, NJ.

STUDYING FOR TESTS

Good Study Habits + Hard Work = Better Grades on Tests

Here are some tips that other *BRAKES* readers
have found successful when studying for tests.

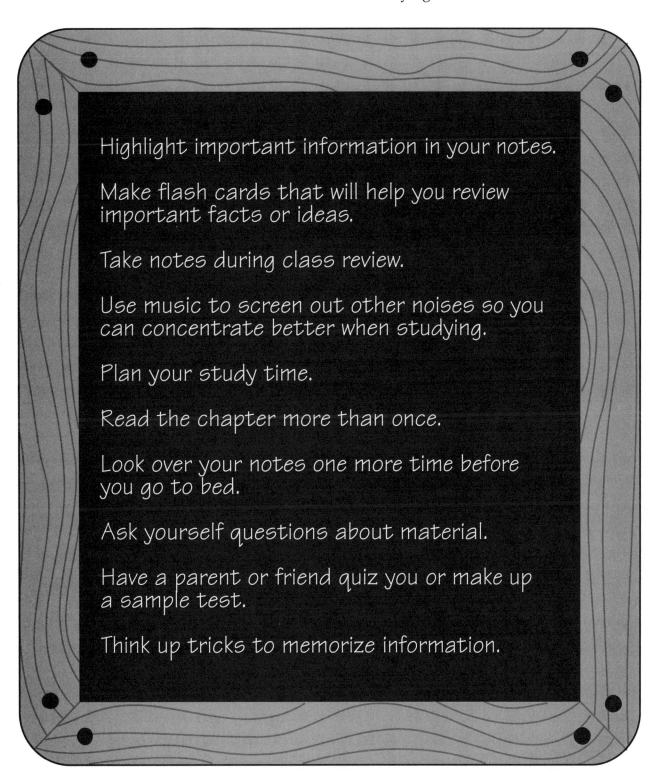

Highlight important information in your notes.

Make flash cards that will help you review important facts or ideas.

Take notes during class review.

Use music to screen out other noises so you can concentrate better when studying.

Plan your study time.

Read the chapter more than once.

Look over your notes one more time before you go to bed.

Ask yourself questions about material.

Have a parent or friend quiz you or make up a sample test.

Think up tricks to memorize information.

DOES THIS SOUND FAMILIAR?

Dear BRAKES,

I have trouble listening and then answering questions in class. My teacher does not understand that someone is making me laugh when she is not looking. She wants to talk to me about this after school, but my mom is waiting to pick me up, so I can't.
What can I do? Thank you.

Adam H., Age 9,
London, Ontario, Canada

Dear Adam,

What a wonderful opportunity to try two different options. First, talk with your teacher. If you are unable to speak with her directly, try writing a note. Tell her what the problem is, what you have tried to do to solve the problem, and then ask her to help you so that you both can get on with your daily activities. Let her know that you would like to speak with her privately during the school day, since your mom is waiting for you after school. Let her know you want to do this as soon as she possibly can so that you can find a solution to your dilemma.

Second, if this does not work, you may have to explain to your mom that you really need to talk to your teacher and you want to do this when the rest of the class is not around. Explain that you want to talk with her face to face, and that you want to ask your teacher how you can solve this problem without making her angry, or getting your classmate in trouble.

Hope these suggestions work. Good luck!

This letter was answered by Mrs. Hinda Lieberman, who is a fourth-grade teacher in Rockville, MD.

WHAT'S WRONG WITH THIS PICTURE?

Let's hope that none of you have ever been in a class like this!
See how many things wrong you can find in this picture.

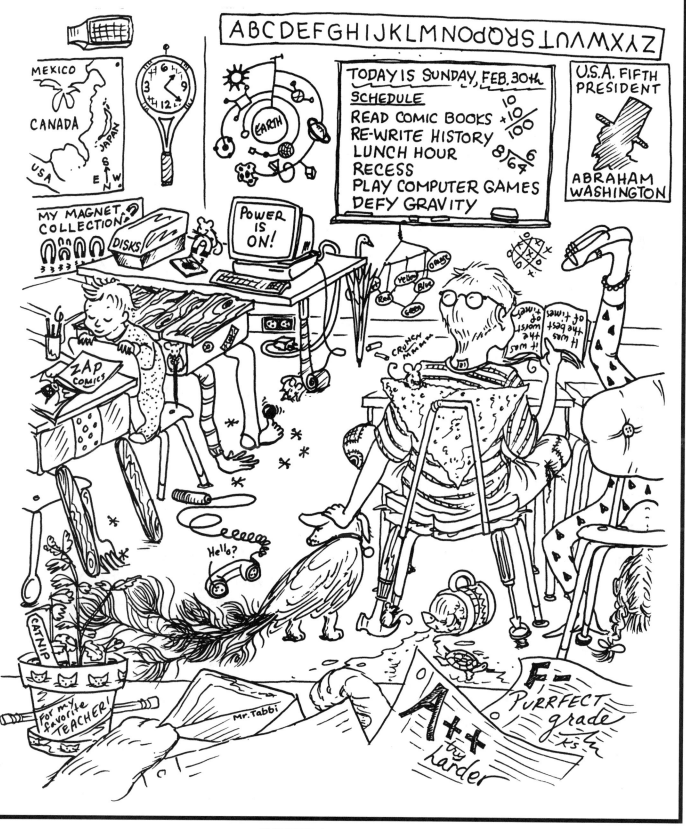

BACKPACK MATCH GAME

Alex and Sam want matching backpacks for school.
Can you help them find two that are the same?

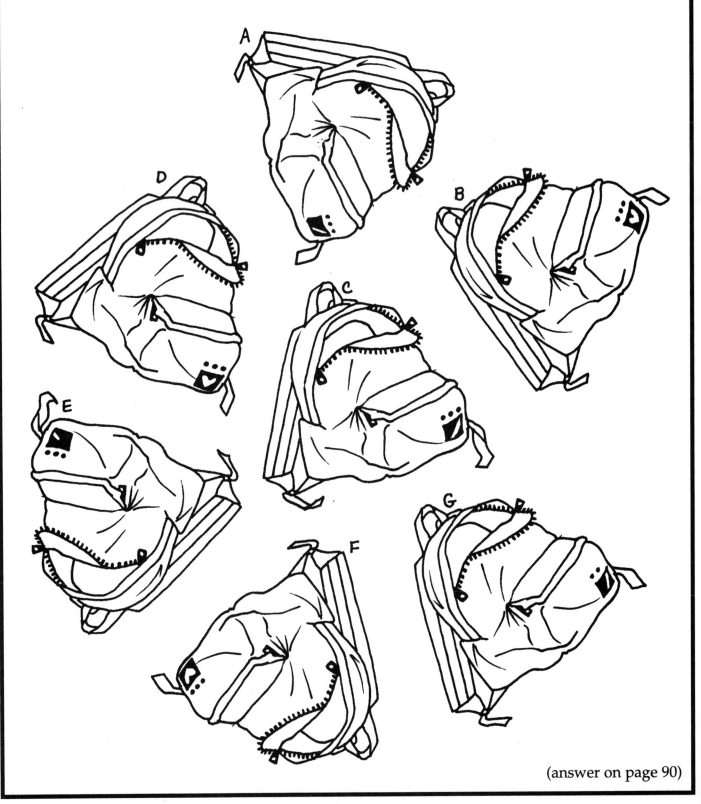

(answer on page 90)

CONQUERING HOMEWORK PROBLEMS

Many kids with ADD tell us that homework is a big problem for them. They forget what they are assigned, forget their books, or lose their homework after they have taken the time to do it. Here are some simple solutions that kids have told us work for them.

PROBLEM:
Not Knowing What Homework Is Assigned

SOLUTION:

Find a homework buddy who will copy the assignments for you. The buddy could use carbon paper to avoid writing it twice.

Ask the teacher to write down the homework for a week or a month at a time. This is especially useful because some kids like to get a head start on assignments over the weekend when they have more time.

PROBLEM:
Forgetting or Losing Your Homework

SOLUTION:

Keep all completed homework in a special section of your notebook.

Make a pocket inside the front cover of your textbook.

Use a special folder just for completed homework. Buy one that is your favorite bright color, or cut out a special picture or draw one on the cover of the folder.

PROBLEM:
Forgetting When Long-Term Assignments Are Due

SOLUTION:

Have your parents give each teacher a set of stamped envelopes addressed to you at home. When the teacher gives out a long-term assignment, ask him or her to drop a copy in the mail to you.

Write all assignments on a large calendar that you keep on the wall of your room at home. Include all due dates. Use different color markers or stickers to call attention to important dates. You can even plan a schedule for completing the various parts of the assignment. TIP: Be sure to build in some time to have the project finished early so you or your teacher can review your work. This usually results in higher grades.

PROBLEM:
Forgetting to Take Home the Necessary Books

SOLUTION:

Buy an extra set of your books to keep at home. Then you will always have them on hand when you need them for assignments. This also has the advantage of allowing you to write or underline in the texts because these books belong to you.

Compare the books that you are putting in your bookbag to take home with the ones that your homework buddy is taking home. This is a good way to ensure that you will have all of the books that you need.

WHAT'S DIFFERENT?

Can you find the ten differences between the first picture
and the second picture? Look closely, as they are very hard to find.

(answer on page 90)

TOOLS FOR SCHOOL

See how many school tools you can find in this word search.
Use the list below.

```
I  E  X  T  R  A  C  R  E  D  I  T  L  Z  Y  X  S
M  W  W  E  K  Q  Q  C  E  X  T  P  E  N  C  I  L
E  R  A  S  E  R  M  G  Q  D  F  A  B  R  O  K  P
D  I  C  T  I  O  N  A  R  Y  L  O  T  U  M  K  V
I  N  F  S  C  N  O  T  E  B  O  O  K  L  P  Z  O
C  S  X  C  N  H  G  E  Q  K  U  I  F  E  A  L  H
I  T  C  P  P  V  O  L  U  N  T  E  E  R  S  S  P
N  R  Y  H  I  G  H  L  I  G  H  T  E  R  S  F  K
E  U  X  L  E  E  S  N  Z  P  Z  Z  G  K  B  N  N
G  M  W  K  P  D  V  B  E  M  I  S  Y  U  A  Z  X
W  E  W  L  V  K  U  T  Y  N  X  O  M  P  M  U  E
W  N  E  E  H  E  W  L  A  K  U  B  S  Y  L  C  C
P  T  V  C  N  F  D  G  E  R  R  A  U  T  N  F  I
S  Z  N  Q  Q  G  R  G  S  E  C  Y  I  Q  O  U  X
J  U  M  P  R  O  P  E  L  K  I  G  T  R  P  H  M
L  Y  K  O  V  E  L  L  R  C  O  Q  Z  E  J  K  O
K  J  S  S  Q  F  A  R  X  Z  M  K  E  D  S  Z  T
```

ATLAS	JUMP ROPE	SCHEDULE
BOOK	KNAPSACK	TEST
COMPASS	LUNCH	UMBRELLA
DICTIONARY	MEDICINE	VOLUNTEER
ERASER	NOTEBOOK	WATCH
FOLDER	ORGANIZER	EXTRA CREDIT
GYM SUIT	PENCIL	YOURSELF
HIGHLIGHTER	QUIZ	ZEAL
INSTRUMENT (musical)	RULER	

(answer on page 91)

MORE HOMEWORK PROBLEMS

Dear BRAKES,

I have trouble doing homework because I always find other things to do at home instead. What should I do?

Shawn C., Age 11

Dear Shawn,

One student we know told us that he makes sure to do his homework at a clean desk in his own room, so when he sits down there is less to distract him. He also turns off all the other lights in the room except for one bright light at his desk so that he stays focused only on the homework there. You could also try to set up a special quiet time in your house each evening so that there will be less noise around you.

Sincerely,
The Editors

Dear Joey,

Maybe you and your mother could try a different plan for the winter months. Some kids spend a few minutes when they first get home working out a homework schedule for the day. If you prove to your mother that you really can complete your homework early each evening, even when you take an hour to play outside in the afternoon, she might be more willing to adjust the homework rules on these short winter days.

Sincerely,
The Editors

Dear BRAKES:

My mom makes me do my homework as soon as I come home from school. In the winter, that means it is dark by the time I finish and I have no time to go outside with my friends. What can I do?

Joey T., Hartford, CT

Can you find these hidden objects?

WAFFLE	**WRENCH**	**FRYING PAN**	**MAN WITH BEARD**
BROOM	**PITCHER**	**PEPPER**	**BOOT**
PENGUIN HEAD	**BUTTERFLY**	**STRAWBERRY**	**HEADPHONES**
CARROT	**MOP**	**PAINT ROLLER**	**BIRD'S NEST**

(answer on page 91)

HAVING FUN! RECREATION & SPORTS

Kids with ADD have to work hard in school each day. If you have trouble staying focused and getting work done, you have to put extra effort into your school day to keep yourself on track. So when you have free time, you really want to enjoy it. After all, people who work hard deserve some time for fun, too! Recreation and sports can be a very important, wonderful part of your life. They provide you with opportunities to use your energy, be creative, explore talents, and have a good time. They also serve as opportunities to learn new ways to concentrate, make friends, and become part of a team. Think about some of the ways you like to spend your free time. You might also want to consider some new activities that will help you develop new skills.

HOW MANY SUMMER FUN WORDS CAN YOU FIND?

```
F B C O R U L Y O T Z O S E I R R E B I
N I A R U F A S O N U L A K E I M O Z R
R K M I P L Y H U M S H O I F A R W L E
I S P O P S G I B O K I S B E V H C L T
L R O W I K S F A Q A X Z R H S B L E A
K E T D E K I H R Z T L C E L K U O H T
B T I B W U Q O B I E E F A N E M O S L
V A C A T I O N E G C L O V A T I P A G
T W W E O M B I Q I O S P K E C R T E F
O N S T R O H S U W E O I S B H A O S N
O K A R G S O P E S V N C K I H S Q U R
F Z E Y R U O R S R O G N O R E L A X U
E I N O U G S A G O L F I K D L E U R B
R N S B N R L I A Q I O C E A N E C S N
A S M H U G L V S Y B M O P N L P R A U
B L I E N E D T E N N I S I M C L A N S
S K Y U R D F I H D Z U S D I V E M D A
M S S L O I N A B U G B I T E U V R A R
E K W L A R H C A E B I M A Y O A Q L R
V U O I A D U G L S I F R E A D R M S E
E L X A M O T O W E L P O N X L T H I F
```

VACATION	PICNIC	BEACH	OCEAN	SHORTS
RUN	SANDALS	BIKE	BARBEQUE	SKATE
SEASHELL	SWIM	TOWEL	HOT	DIVE
SUNBURN	GOLF	SKETCH	CAMP	RIDE
RAIN	FISH	ICE CREAM	HIKE	BERRIES
TENNIS	SLEEP	WATER SKI	BAREFOOT	READ
BUG BITE	TRAVEL	HAT	FAN	SUNGLASSES
FLOWER	PLAY	RELAX	LAKE	POOL

(answer on page 91)

TURTLE BEACH MAZE

Here is a great exercise to help you practice concentrating!
Can you help this girl reach her dog,
Pepper, by taking her through the maze?

HAVE YOURSELF SOME FUN!

Do you ever dream of being on stage or in a movie? Why not put on a play with your friends? The stage can be in your basement or living room, and the props and costumes can be fun to improvise. Your public library should have plenty of good plays. Or write your own! Remember that it does not need to be anything fancy to be fun.

Do you enjoy the water? You may not think about swimming during the winter months, but an indoor community pool offers fun in the water all year long.

Do you like sports? Most communities offer recreation league or weekend intramural sports such as baseball, bowling, basketball, and soccer. Or call some friends and get your own game going.

Gardening is America's number one recreational activity. Indoors, it is fun to plant seeds and watch them grow. Do you like flowers and vegetables? Try out your green thumb by growing some in a sunny garden outside. Or inside, start your own miniature greenhouse by using a clean fish tank.

Remember, even when daylight hours are shorter in winter, there is still plenty to do to keep your body and mind active. Hobbies and play are just as important as your schoolwork. So plan your time wisely and leave room for the things you like to do.

April Moore is a freelance writer and editor living in the Shenandoah Valley in Virginia.

GOING CAMPING

Can you find these hidden objects in this illustration?

HEAD OF LETTUCE	HORSESHOE CRAB	NEWT
SAILBOAT	BEAVER	TOY CAR
FLASHLIGHT	SKULL	TWO TEETH
PENGUIN	OLD SHOE	EMU
SEA LION	CONCH SHELL	BLUE CRAB

(answer on page 91)

VISIT MT. FUN LODGE

You need to relax? Take a visit to Mt. Fun Lodge and see
if you can locate the following buried objects:

BUTTON   SLICE OF PIE   RED PEPPER   HOCKEY STICK
WHALE   ROCKET SHIP   TOOTH   SQUIRREL
POLAR BEAR   OCTOPUS   HANGER   SAFETY PIN
PORCUPINE   STRAWBERRY   DUCK   MOOSE

(answer on page 92)

BOOKS CROSSWORD PUZZLE

"Reading: What a Nice Way to Spend Some Time!"

The clues in this puzzle are about books that you might have read, or books that other members of your family may know about. See how many answers you can find.

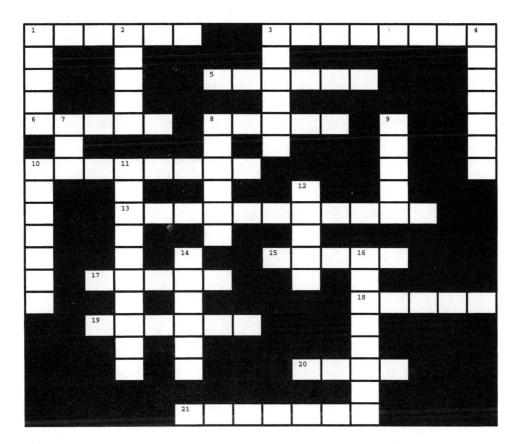

Across

1. _ _ _ _ _ _ is the name of the pig in *Charlotte's Web*.
3. A table of _ _ _ _ _ _ _ _ is always in the front of the book.
5. The name of Ramona's sister.
6. R.L. _ _ _ _ _ is the author of the "Goosebumps" series.
8. A long running series about two boys who solve mysteries, The _ _ _ _ _ Boys.
10. A popular book is *The Lion, the Witch and the* _ _ _ _ _ _ _ _.
13. Matt _ _ _ _ _ _ _ _ _ _ _ is a writer of children's sports books.
15. Roald Dahl wrote *James and the Giant* _ _ _ _ _.
17. A classic book about four sisters that was written by Louisa May Alcott: *Little* _ _ _ _ _ .
18. You will find this in the back of a book.
19. Aesop was known for writing _ _ _ _ _ _.
20. A book that a person writes about him or herself is an _ _ _ biography.
21. A book that is not true.

Down

1. In a book written by Thomas Rockwell, Billy made a bet and had to eat fifteen fried _ _ _ _ _ .
2. *Encyclopedia* _ _ _ _ _, *Kid Detective*.
3. *Dear Mr. Henshaw* and *The Mouse and the Motorcycle* were written by Beverly _ _ _ _ _ _.
4. A type of fantasy book: _ _ _ _ _ _ _- fiction.
7. In *Alice in Wonderland*, Alice went to a _ _ _ party.
8. *The* _ _ _ _ _ _ was written by J. R. R. Tolkien.
9. Judy _ _ _ _ _ wrote many books including *Freckle Juice* and *Superfudge*.
10. _ _ _ _ _ _ _ *School is Falling Down* was written by Louis Sachar.
11. A book used to find the meaning of words.
12. "You can't tell a book by its _ _ _ _ _."
14. The color of the brick road in *The Wizard of Oz*.
16. The author of *Jurassic Park* is Michael _ _ _ _ _ _ _ _.

(answer on page 92)

BORED AT HOME

Boredom doesn't only strike at school. It can attack anywhere, anytime. Here are some ways you can keep boredom under control at home:

- Daydream, daydream, daydream. Give yourself permission to think about your future, remember your past, and enjoy things that you like about the present. Let your mind wander, create a fantasy story, include your friends and family, and take everyone someplace where you have never been before.

- Getting back to earth, think of different ways to do your chores. If you have to mow the lawn, try doing it in circles instead of straight lines (with permission of course). When you clean up your room, try doing part of it as fast as possible like the "Six Million Dollar Man." Then try doing part of it as slowly as possible, like you are in slow motion.

- See how many details you can notice in your day-to-day life. How does the silverware feel when you're setting the table? How do different spices smell? What color are your best friend's eyes?

- Team up with a friend and become one another's boredom buddy. Create a long-term anti-boredom project that either of you can turn to in case of boredom emergencies. Build a tree house, write and illustrate a book together, or make your own video. Interview your boredom buddy or other friends about anything that comes to mind.

- Make a mental list of your favorite words. "Pomegranate" is one of ours.

- Explore the world with a computer. Try out a new game, learn how to use a new piece of software, or surf the Internet. Write e-mail to people who live in other parts of the world and ask them questions about what they do when they get bored.

- Go rollerblading, skateboarding, running, or even for a walk. Play basketball. Hop on your bike and go for a ride. Exercise releases chemicals in your brain that help you feel better. Did you ever notice that sometimes when you are doing physical work or play, you come up with great ideas?

Being bored is a natural part of ADD. Staying bored is a matter of choice. And by the way, we looked it up: A gerund is a verb that ends in "-ing," like walking, talking, and ... ending.

This article is contributed by Carlos Pedraza (Portland, ME) and Felice Kaufman (Bethesda, MD), independent consultants in gifted education.

EVERYBODY LOVES FREE TIME!!

How do you feel when you have an entire weekend ahead of you,
or a day off from school? Find the items that have to do
with what these kids may come across during their free time.
See if you can find these:

COMPUTER	SHIP	STRAW HAT	GUINEA PIG
FLOWER POT	POPSICLE STICK	BRACELET	PALM TREE
FISH	CHESS PIECE	LETTER "Z"	CATERPILLAR
PAPER AIRPLANE	BOOK	LIGHT BULB	RABBIT

CAMPING QUEST

See how many camp words you can find.
Some words may be backwards or upside down.

AIR MATTRESS   BACKPACK   BLANKET   BOOTS
BUG SPRAY   CAMERA   CANTEEN   COOLER
DRINKS   FISHING POLE   FLASHLIGHT   FOOD
MARSHMALLOWS   LANTERN   MATCHES   SLEEPING BAG
RAIN GEAR   SOAP   STOVE   TENT
     TOWEL   WATER

```
B  L  A  N  K  E  T  S  S  T  O  O  B  Y  K  B
D  R  I  N  K  S  L  E  E  P  I  N  G  B  A  G
O  P  B  M  F  F  L  Y  N  X  A  B  E  H  S  L
O  X  P  J  W  R  G  Y  X  T  C  O  O  L  E  R
F  L  A  S  H  L  I  G  H  T  K  A  S  Q  F  D
I  A  I  L  E  J  L  B  V  G  I  B  M  K  Y  C
S  K  R  G  W  A  T  E  R  A  I  N  G  E  A  R
H  O  M  A  R  S  H  M  A  L  L  O  W  S  R  R
I  V  A  T  Y  R  B  K  H  S  T  O  V  E  P  A
N  G  T  L  K  C  Y  M  A  O  E  W  T  H  S  G
G  J  T  R  X  A  J  S  W  T  O  V  D  C  G  H
P  E  R  L  A  N  T  E  R  N  A  W  K  T  U  V
O  C  E  R  C  T  L  K  C  A  P  K  C  A  B  R
L  H  S  D  R  E  H  L  F  G  M  L  I  M  P  M
E  M  S  K  E  E  X  C  E  P  P  M  Z  Z  Q
P  E  P  V  J  N  E  W  C  N  H  A  N  Y  X  N
```

(answer on page 92)

SPORTSMANSHIP

Is Not ...

intimidating
boasting
taunting
booing
gritting
trash talking
parents & coaches yelling
hot dogging
coaches demeaning players
players "dissing" coaches
cheating to win
win-lose
about money
doing the popular thing
inciting the crowd
pushing down
fighting correction
"I"

Is ...

congratulating
complimenting
thanking
celebrating
smiling
not talking
cheering for all the players
sharing the ball
coaches teaching players
players respecting coaches
competing honestly
win-win
about values
doing the right thing
focusing on the game
helping up
accepting criticism
"We"

Sportsmanship is:

shaking hands after the game
understanding that an opponent is not an enemy
recognizing a "nice play" by the other team
playing by the "spirit" of the rule
congratulating the winner and the loser

Sportmanship is shown not by the score,
but by how you played the game.

This article is by Bob Wagner, Boys' Basketball Coach, Washington, DC.

HIKING MAZE

Bob, Betty, and Grandpa have just arrived at the entrance to "Brakes Park." Help them find their way to "Owl Ridge Campsite" through the maze of streams, paths, waterfalls, and mountains without crossing over any lines.

TAKING YOUR MEDICATION WITH YOU

Dear BRAKES:

I'm going to overnight camp for the first time this summer. Should I take my Ritalin while I'm there?

Greg, Age 9
California

Dear Greg:

If you need your medication to be in control of your behaviors, pay attention, and enjoy yourself, then by all means discuss with your parents taking your medicine with you to camp. You should also bring along a written schedule with the name of your medicine, and the time and amount of each dose that you take. Have your parents send enough medication to last the entire camp session. Make sure that the camp counselor and nurse know how important it is for you to take your medicine on time. Have fun!

Sincerely,
The Editors

25 THINGS TO DO INSTEAD OF WATCHING T.V.

15 WAYS
TO BRIGHTEN YOUR DAY

When people take time to do things they like, they enjoy life and feel good about themselves. Here are some ideas that you might like to try to make any day special. Add your own favorites at the bottom of the page.

1. Go for a walk.

2. Say something nice to someone else.

3. Watch a funny movie.

4. Tell a friend a joke.

5. Call a relative who thinks you're neat.

6. Listen to music you like.

7. Get a hug or give yourself one.

8. Sing a song or whistle.

9. Give yourself a compliment.

10. Wear your favorite shirt.

11. Read a joke book.

12. Have an ice cream cone with a friend.

13. Smile!

14. Play with your pet.

15. Ask your parents to tell you a story about when you were little.

Write your own ideas here.

HOW TO KEEP COOL IN THE SUMMER

Here is a list of some really "cool" summertime suggestions from three kids who live in Tucson, Arizona. The average summer temperature in Tucson is 86 degrees, which means that on many days the temperature reaches 100 degrees or more. It may not get as hot in the summer where you live as it does in Tucson, but their ideas are great fun anyway.

Swim in the pool for one hour.

Stay inside until 3 p.m. if it gets to be 109 degrees or above.

Play with my water gun shooter against my brother.

Have a sprinkler relay with my friends.

Go to swim lessons.

Play water hose tag.

Go to the park and have water balloon fights.

Picnic outside in the morning when the sun rises,

and have ice cream in the evening.

Ice and popsicles can also keep you cool.

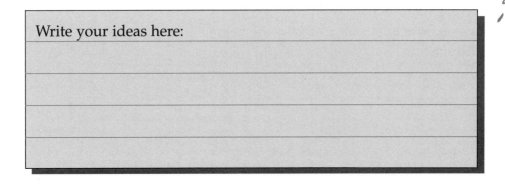

Write your ideas here:

GOOD SPORTS

Many kids with ADD report being good at sports.
This is a good way to stay physically fit, make friends,
and use up excess energy. See how many kinds of sports equipment
you can find hidden in the picture below.

GOLF BALL	HOCKEY STICK	HAND WEIGHT
KAYAK	ICE SKATE	OAR
BOOMERANG	PENNANT	GOLF TEE
ROLLERBLADE	WHISTLE	HOCKEY PUCK
FOOTBALL	MAN WITH HEADPHONES	BOWLING PIN
	LACROSSE STICK	

(answer on page 92)

YOUR SPECIALTIES

Everyone is unique in his or her own way.
Circle your specialties from the list below.
They all add up to a SPECIAL you!

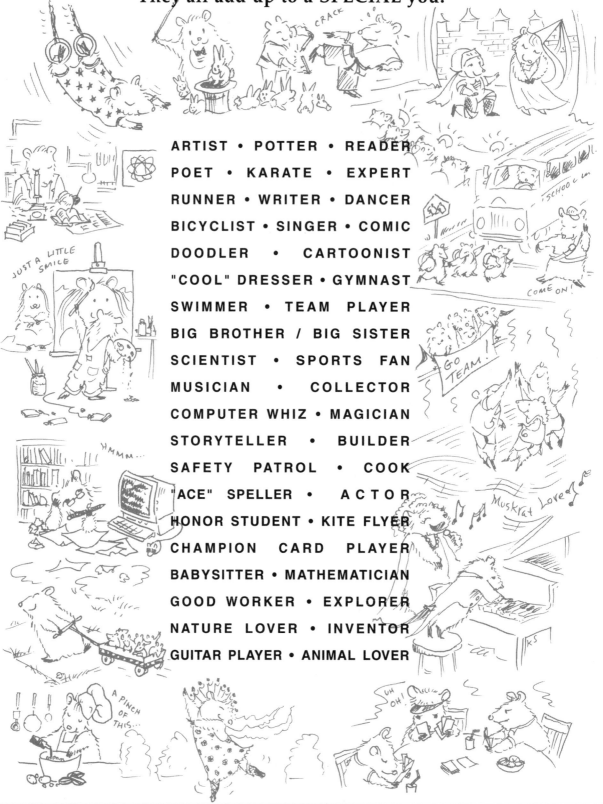

ARTIST • POTTER • READER
POET • KARATE • EXPERT
RUNNER • WRITER • DANCER
BICYCLIST • SINGER • COMIC
DOODLER • CARTOONIST
"COOL" DRESSER • GYMNAST
SWIMMER • TEAM PLAYER
BIG BROTHER / BIG SISTER
SCIENTIST • SPORTS FAN
MUSICIAN • COLLECTOR
COMPUTER WHIZ • MAGICIAN
STORYTELLER • BUILDER
SAFETY PATROL • COOK
"ACE" SPELLER • ACTOR
HONOR STUDENT • KITE FLYER
CHAMPION CARD PLAYER
BABYSITTER • MATHEMATICIAN
GOOD WORKER • EXPLORER
NATURE LOVER • INVENTOR
GUITAR PLAYER • ANIMAL LOVER

SPORTS CROSSWORD PUZZLE

Name the sport or activity that is closely identified with many of the clues.

Across

1. This sport uses a puck.
4. Gear needed to swim under water.
6. With clue 10 across, Kristi Yamaguchi's specialty.
8. Greg Lougainis was an Olympic _ _ _ _ _ .
10. Frozen water.
11. Top award is the World Cup.
12. One in the gutter doesn't count.
14. To canter is one kind of _ _ _ _ _ _.
15. Give a _ _ _ _ !
16. Specialty of Dominique Dawes.
18. Used in many sports and comes in all sizes.
20. Two paddles are standard equipment in this sport.
24. Only the putter can be used on this playing area.
25. The winning prize here is a gold medal.
27. _ _ _ _ball is Joe Montana's sport.

Down

2. A black belt tops out this sport.
3. Wimbledon is one setting.
5. Babe Ruth's sport, with clue 18 across.
6. Breast stroke, for example.
7. You spike this, with clue 18 across.
9. Jackie Joyner-Kersee is well known in this sport.
12. George Foreman is tops here.
13. You use a wood or an iron.
17. A chair lift brings you to new heights for this sport.
19. The fastest downhill slide at the Olympics.
21. Either water or a cue stick works here.
22. Where you go for phys ed classes.
23. Michael Jordan used to fly high in this sport, with clue 18 across.
26. A small ball easily goes _ _ _ _ a large net.

(answers on page 93)

MAKING AND KEEPING FRIENDS

Everybody wants to have friends, but making friends and keeping them is not always easy for kids with ADD. Friendships take work and planning, like other important things such as homework or getting ready for camp. With practice, making a friend can become easier. To get started, try eating lunch together or playing at recess or after school. In this section, we have presented things to do with your friends, as well as skills you may want to practice to make you a better friend. You will also find some hints on what to do about teasing.

Some children with ADD may have behaviors that make it harder for them to be good friends. But it is possible to work out the problems and learn how to make and keep friends. There are special friends out there for everyone.

HIDE AND SEEK

Finding a friend is not always easy, but if you
persist and look all around, you might find
one where you least expect it.
Find ten friends who are hiding in the forest.

WHAT TO DO ABOUT TEASING

Kids with ADD sometimes have trouble controlling their behavior. Sometimes their behavior causes them to be teased by others. Teasing can hurt. These are some ideas suggested by kids on how to get along better with others.

Here are some basic rules about when to tease and how to know when to stop.

- Tease only when you and the "teasee" know that this is really just for fun.
- Be aware of how others react. Sometimes a person's body language will tell you it is time to stop long before their words will.
- Know when it is time to stop. Not everybody can take teasing.

Here are some basic rules to prevent you from being teased because you have ADD.

- Keep your emotions in check. React calmly. Try not to overreact or cry in front of others.
- Look others straight in the eyes and tell them how you feel.
- Treat yourself with respect and others will respect you.
- Maintain good posture and carry your body with confidence, so that people see you do respect yourself.
- Use a calm, gentle tone of voice when talking and others will do the same.
- Be a good listener. A good friend knows when to stop talking and listen.
- Go with the flow. Sometimes you have to give up some things to get other things.
- MYOB. This means mind your own business. If someone is having problems behaving, let an adult control him or her.
- Have a sense of humor about yourself.
- Whenever possible, play with kids who you know like you.

Here are some suggestions about how to react if you are teased.

- Laugh it off.
- Walk away. Say, "I'm out of here. See ya."
- Ignore behavior you don't enjoy. Involve yourself in something else.
- Go with the flow. "Tell me something I haven't heard before," you might say.
- Ask a distracting question to change the subject, such as, "Do you know the time?"
- Find someone to hook up with that you consider a friend.
- Acknowledge mistakes and move on. "You're right, I blew it. Next time I won't do it."
- If physically threatened or harassed, tell an adult.
- Say the obvious. "You're kicking my chair."
- If others are whispering about you, say quietly and firmly, "Did you have something you wanted to say about me?"
- Say nothing. Do nothing when teased.

If you can read and follow this advice, you will find that you won't be teased as much and you will also have a better understanding of what it feels like when you tease someone else.

This article is contributed by Cathi Cohen, LCSW, who is a social worker and the Director of Stepping Stones, a social skills group therapy program for children in Fairfax, VA.

THINGS TO DO WITH FRIENDS

OUTDOORS

- Play soccer but use a tennis ball or football instead.
- Start a collection of rocks, bugs, or flowers.
- Go on a scavenger hunt to find something that starts with each letter of the alphabet, such as a = acorn, b = bug, c = caterpillar, etc.
- Make a fort; in winter use snow, in fall use leaves, and in summer use old blankets or sheets.
- Organize a jump rope contest.
- Look for pictures in the clouds.
- Paint a mural using old sheets or large pieces of cardboard. Be sure to ask for permission first.

INDOORS

- Use the lid of a box to make up a maze, using straws, ping-pong balls, and cardboard.
- Ask your parents for old socks, yarn, and scraps of material to design your own puppets.
- Fingerprint with whipped cream or chocolate pudding. Get your parent's permission first!
- Write a short play together and rehearse it. Then perform it for younger brothers and sisters or neighbors.
- Draw or paint your own greeting cards. Make a bunch, so you have one when you need one.
- With a friend, start a collection — such as stamps, photos, or baseball cards — and work on it when you get together.

NOBODY'S PERFECT: SOLVING PROBLEMS WITH YOUR FRIENDS

Knowing how to resolve problems is important for keeping up good friendships. Here are two examples of problems that might arise. How would you handle each one?

Problem #1

Choose the solution you like best!

Problem #2

Janine is a ten-year-old girl who has a good friend named Cindy. Although they really like each other, when they get together they often get into arguments. It is hard for them to agree on what they want to do, so they spend a lot of time talking about it and getting annoyed with each other.

Which of these could be good solutions to their problem?

- Ask their parents for a suggestion each time they play.
- Make a list of things they both enjoy. Choose a different activity each time they get together.
- Take turns deciding what to do that day.
- Argue until one of them gives up.
- Other ideas:

FRIENDS SEE EACH OTHER AS SPECIAL!!!

Color this!

QUALITIES OF A GOOD FRIEND

Are you a good friend? Circle the words that describe you.
Think of your friends. Write the name of a friend next to
the quality that describes him or her.

HONEST _____

HELPFUL _____

CARING _____

SYMPATHETIC _____

FLEXIBLE _____

FUN _____

CREATIVE _____

ENERGETIC _____

CONSIDERATE _____

HUMOROUS _____

RELIABLE _____

THOUGHTFUL _____

GENEROUS _____

LOOKING AT FEELINGS

Feelings are an important part of who you are. They can get you into trouble or help you enjoy life. It is important that you learn to recognize your feelings and learn how to deal with them. Some of the activities in this section are designed to help you do just that. Kids with ADD may at times feel overloaded, frustrated, or angry. On the next pages, you will find some tips to help you deal with negative feelings and better appreciate the many positive feelings you can also experience.

FACES AND FEELINGS

Look at each of the faces on this page.
Pay special attention to the feelings on each person's face.
Match the faces with the sentences describing each feeling.

1. I'm so worried. What if I lose my job?
2. That is the most disgusting thing I have ever smelled. It makes me feel sick.
3. Don't tell George about the surprise party we're planning for Saturday night.
4. If you ever do that again, I will be really angry!
5. Thank you so much for letting me hug your new rabbit. It felt so soft and warm.
6. Oh, no! I forgot to feed my dog before I left for school today!
7. I'm sort of shy, so it's hard for me to be in this big room full of people I don't know.
8. If this class doesn't get more interesting very soon, I will fall asleep!

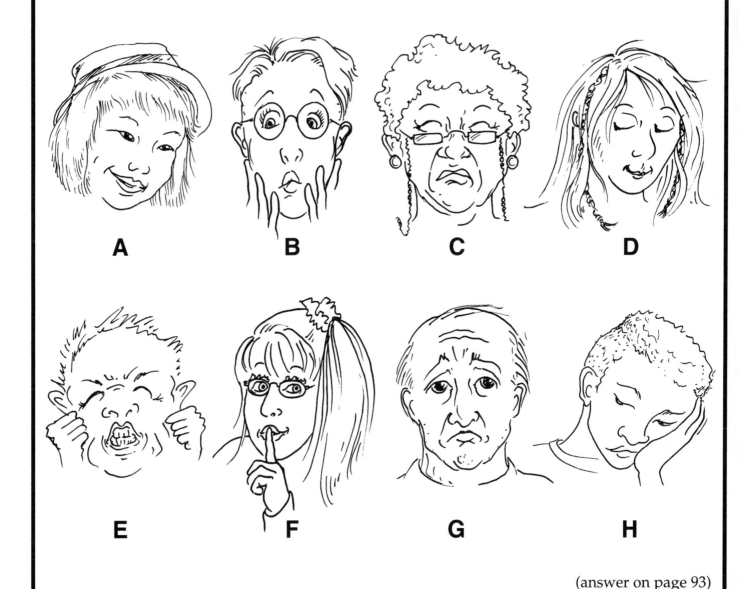

A   B   C   D

E   F   G   H

(answer on page 93)

OH FRUSTRATIONS!

They are a part of everyone's life, but a sense of humor goes a long way toward getting you through. Marty Berger from Silver Spring, Maryland, has put together this list of frustrations that could make anyone groan!

- You arrive at the airport exactly on time, then realize that you forgot to set your watch ahead for Daylight Savings Time.

- Your parents make a wrong turn on the highway at rush hour.

- The fast food restaurant clerk has to be called three times just to take your order.

- There is a direct relationship between how late you are, and how slow traffic is.

- The book you need at the library is out.

- You send a small tomato into orbit trying to cut it.

- You have a coughing fit while you are observing at the Supreme Court.

- You fly to Chicago, but your luggage goes to Brazil.

- You develop eyestrain from trying to read the nutrition information on a product.

HOW DO YOU FEEL?

Kids with ADD have all kinds of feelings.
Circle the feelings that you have sometimes. At the bottom of the
page, there is room for you to add other feelings that you have had.
Share this page with your parent, teacher, or counselor.

ENERGETIC	HUMOROUS	FORGETFUL
UNPOPULAR	ATHLETIC	IMAGINATIVE
CREATIVE	IMPATIENT	ENTHUSIASTIC
SENSITIVE	SCARED	ADAPTABLE
ATTRACTIVE	HAPPY	DUMB
TEASED	SMART	CONFUSED
FRIENDLY	OVERLOADED	ANXIOUS
ANGRY	CARING	DISORGANIZED
CURIOUS	FRUSTRATED	TENSE
MISUNDERSTOOD	SPECIAL	HYPER
ARTISTIC	PICKED ON	SILLY

_____

_____

_____

_____

From The "Putting on the Brakes" Activity Book for Young People With ADHD,
*by Patricia O. Quinn and Judith M. Stern, published by Magination Press, Washington, DC, 1993.
Reprinted with permission.*

SUPER WORD SEARCH

Can you find all of the words in the list on page 64?
To make it harder, there are a number of words that are backwards
or upside down.

```
C O N F U S E D E R A C S P E C I A L
F R U S T R A T E D Y K E M U G X P F
O V E R L O A D E D P R N C A R I N G
R C N A X B W A C B P P S U N R W N W
G I T V T C O E F T A N I R X K T K T
E T H U Y I R E P Y H N T I I D C M E
T E U X V B V G K D U C I O O X J O F
F L S P N Q L E M N M I V U U B M U D
U H I T P I C K E D O N E S S X Y N I
L T A M I S U N D E R S T O O D R S S
T A S F A I L H C S O Q Q K T A R C O
B R T D R G M T A A U N P O P U L A R
O T I F T I I P U E S E J G T I G R G
Z I C U P E E N A T T R A C T I V E A
R S F C D C N N A T J X B J X K K D N
M T J X W K G S D T I G O E A X C G I
C I T E G R E N E L I E I Z Y J Q E Z
M C C E Y Y G J P T Y V N P K L V X E
F G Z C A D A P T A B L E T X O D T D
```

(answer on page 93)

WHAT'S IN A FACE?

The next time you watch television, turn off the sound and look carefully at the actors. Can you tell how they are feeling by looking at their faces and how they use their bodies? Compare your guesses with those of your parents or friends who are watching with you.

Take some empty index cards. Have an adult write down one feeling on each card. Try to act out that feeling without speaking. See if a friend or family member can guess the different feelings you are trying to express. (This can get pretty funny!)

These activities are helpful in learning how to understand other people's emotions and feelings. Friendship really begins when you can understand how someone else feels. Being able to "read" their expressions can go a long way in improving a friendship.

Sad

Happy

Angry

YOUR ANGRY FEELINGS

Dear BRAKES:

In school I sometimes get frustrated and lose my temper. Then the other kids make fun and laugh at me. What should I do?

JR

Dear JR:

Here are some ideas to try when you begin to feel angry in school. Slow down by taking a deep breath. Some kids find it helpful to close their eyes and count to ten. Others picture a STOP sign in their head. This reminds them to have better control. You also might try talking to yourself in order to calm down. Say things that you find reassuring or that just make you feel better. Try talking to your teacher about what frustrates you and creates the problem in the first place.

Sincerely,
The Editors

Dear BRAKES,

I have been getting very angry almost every day. Can you tell me what to do about this?

Gary S., age 10, Harrisburg, PA

Dear Gary,

It is always important to acknowledge what you are feeling. In your case, it is important to try to get to the reasons why you are feeling angry in order to take an active role in doing something about it. You need to look at the situations or the times that cause you to feel angry. Talk to the people involved to see if you can change these triggers; for example, if you are angry because you are always last in line at school, talk to the teacher about allowing you to be first on occasion. It is important to try to avoid those situations that make you angry, if you can. If you usually get into a fight with your brother or sister when you sit together in the back of the car, maybe you could take turns sitting alone in the front seat.

There are several techniques that people can use when they feel they are getting angry so that they do not lose control. The most common one is counting to ten slowly. You can also close your eyes and imagine a big red STOP sign, or "take a quick trip" to a scene in your mind that helps you feel calmer.

Finally, if you feel that you are often out of control and nothing is working, be sure to talk to an adult. Seeing a counselor and talking about your feelings may be just what you need to get started on the right road again.

Sincerely,
The Editors

Dear BRAKES:

My name is Jamie and I have ADD. I have a lot of problems with anger. In school, when I get angry I break a pencil and my anger is out. What can I do at home?

Dear Jamie:

There are lots of things you might try at home to control your anger. Here are a few suggestions. Pick one and see if it works for you. If that one doesn't work out too well, try another. Keep trying and don't give up. You'll be glad that you did. You'll like yourself better, and people will like being around you.

- Try counting to 10, slowly breathing in and out.
- Get a punching bag or a pillow to punch when you are angry.
- Start singing your favorite song. It's hard to be angry when you are singing.
- Ask a parent to get a bunch of nails, some wood, and a hammer. Go pound nails when you are angry. Soon you'll forget what you were angry about.
- Take a jog or a run.
- Go to your room or someplace else where you can be by yourself until you calm down. Then you can return to the situation that made you angry and handle it the right way.

Keep trying! Don't give up or give in to your anger.

Sincerely,
The Editors

YOUR FAMILY AND YOU

Families are an important part of our lives. We learn from them, play with them, and receive help and support from them. Families cry and laugh together. Although being a member of a family can sometimes be difficult, most children are happy to have people in their lives to make them feel special.

Your family goes beyond just the people who live in your house. You may have other relatives who live nearby or far away. Take advantage of the qualities that your different family members each possess. If you have an aunt who likes to talk, call her up when you have something important to share. If your big sister is a math genius, ask her for help with homework that you cannot do alone. If your grandfather likes to build things, maybe he would enjoy helping you with a Scout project. Kids with ADD may need extra support to accomplish their goals. So look around at those who love you and see all the people who are there to help.

WHAT'S DIFFERENT?

Can you find what is different between the top picture
and the bottom picture that made Mom so happy?

TIPS FOR REMEMBERING

Dear J.V.,

We are sorry to hear that having ADD is not fun for you and causes some problems. But you have already taken the first step to making things better by asking for help. You have also done a good job in identifying what the problems are. We suggest that you have a talk with your parents and try to work out some good solutions. Let them know that you are not forgetting on purpose and that you would like some help. Making lists or having your parents write reminders on a wipe-off board on the wall can help you remember.

Dear BRAKES,

I am having problems obeying my mom and dad. ADD is not very fun for me. I have a short memory, and sometimes I forget what Mom and Dad say for me to do. Sometimes in school, I get a lot of homework and I have trouble concentrating long enough to get it done. Will you please try to help me?

J.V., age 8, Michigan

You can also ask your parents to just give you one direction or task at a time and wait until you finish before giving you another. Brightly colored notes that you can stick on doors or your wall may be helpful. Tying a ribbon or colored string around something or attaching it to your wrist or clothing can help you to remember that you are supposed to do something.

Good luck and have fun coming up with other solutions.

Sincerely,
The Editors

WHAT DO I DO NOW?

Look at these problems. Try to think of some good solutions.

I got really muddy making the game's winning catch. So Mom put my uniform in the wash with my red socks.

It turned PINK!!

HELP!!!!

Your solution ... Write and/or illustrate.

It took me 6 months to save up enough money to get the game CD I really wanted.

Now my brother wants to play it for FREE?!!

Your solution ... Write and/or illustrate.

INVENT YOUR OWN SOLUTION

Someone took my new rollerblades.

It was my sister!

She fell and broke her leg. It hurts.

What do I do now?

Your solution ... Write and/or illustrate.

We couldn't decide where to go for dinner.

So we took a vote. Chinese food won. I lost.

I don't want to go.

Your solution ... Write and/or illustrate.

FAMILY PROBLEMS

Dear BRAKES:

My mom thinks that I'm never paying attention, even when I am, so she says things about a thousand times to me. Help!

Maria H., Age 10, Maine

Dear BRAKES:

My brother is always hitting me. What should I do?

Mindy L., Age 7, Delaware

Dear Maria:

Remember: eye contact. When your mom tells you to do something, look her straight in the eye and say "uh-huh" or "yes" two or three times. If she still repeats herself, say politely, "I heard you, Mom." It's important for people to know that they have been heard and understood. Two good things will happen. First, by using this technique, you stay focused. Second, your mother will be thrilled because you do what she asks you to do!

Sincerely,
The Editors

Dear Mindy,

First, try to talk with your brother and tell him how you feel. Ask if something is bothering him that you could do something about. If this doesn't work, you need to get an adult involved so that the hitting will stop.

Sincerely,
The Editors

MY FAMILY TREE

Everyone is part of a larger family. Finding out more about your relatives is fun and can sometimes uncover very interesting information about your family. As you fill in this Family Tree, ask about other family members who might have some of the same qualities you have. Some examples would be: red hair, tall or short height, good athletic skills, a sense of humor, artistic talent, and forgetfulness.

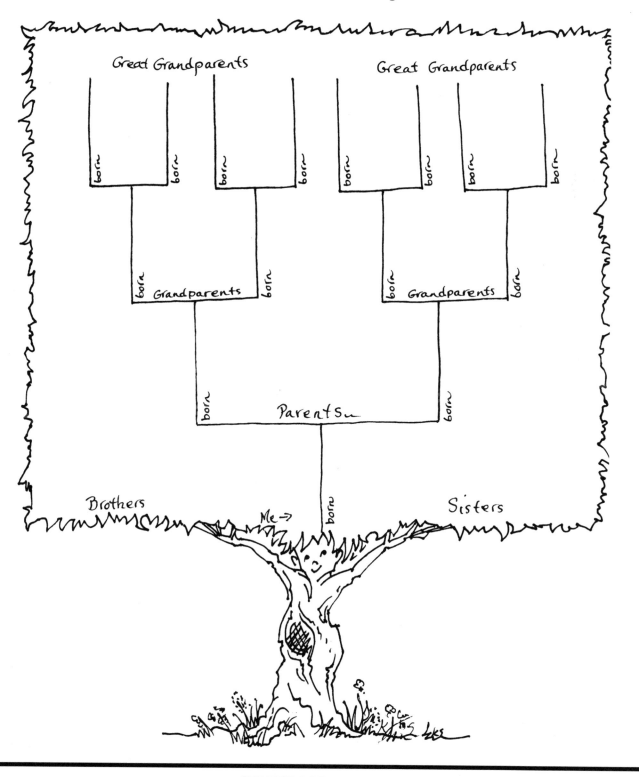

FIND THE RELATIVES

When you need help, want to share a joke, show off a good grade, or find a missing shoe, your relatives are there to make life a little easier. Find the names of family members hidden in this word search.

Here are the words to look for:

AUNT	BROTHER	COUSIN	DAD
DAUGHTER	GRANDFATHER	GRANDMOTHER	KIDS
MOM	NEPHEW	NIECE	PARENTS
PETS	SIBLING	SISTER	SON
STEPFATHER	STEPMOTHER	TWIN	UNCLE

```
H   S   T   E   P   F   A   T   H   E   R   P   I   N   P   Z
K   I   I   T   W   I   N   I   E   C   E   S   D   A   D   E
T   B   K   S   T   E   P   M   O   T   H   E   R   D   H   O
P   L   H   F   T   Y   E   U   S   O   N   E   P   H   E   W
K   I   D   S   B   E   S   H   H   U   N   C   L   E   W   E
D   N   A   L   P   I   R   E   T   T   J   T   N   U   A   V
I   G   U   C   N   L   Y   G   S   T   H   U   W   M   D   K
S   J   G   R   A   N   D   F   A   T   H   E   R   S   R   Q
R   E   H   T   O   R   B   Q   X   G   G   B   J   N   B   Y
S   H   T   N   M   Q   S   N   M   C   N   S   E   F   X   O
N   T   E   U   Q   O   P   B   P   M   M   L   K   B   E   O
X   G   R   A   N   D   M   O   T   H   E   R   E   W   F   Z
```

(answer on page 93)

FAMILY FUN

Imagine that your parents have asked you to do the planning for a whole day of family fun. What would you decide to do together?

Design your own FUN DAY with your family. You can write or draw a picture of what your day would include. (Yes, you do have to include your little brother!)

Here are some ideas that kids have shared with us.

For a day of family fun, I would want to go to Nauticus, a place where you learn about sea life. For dinner we would go to my favorite restaurant where they cook the food in front of your face. Then I would take our two puppies for a long walk. The last thing I would want to do is go see a movie together.

James B.
Age 9
Georgia

If I had the whole day with my family, we would sleep late then play on computers. We would all go helmet diving in the ocean. We would touch a moray eel. Then we would take home the eel to be a family pet!

Max B.
Age 8
Virginia

A FAMILY CELEBRATES SPECIAL TIMES TOGETHER

This family is celebrating a big snowfall by building a "Snowfamily" together. They have hidden many objects that are used in different kinds of family celebrations. Some of these are: weddings, birthdays, Christmas, Easter, Hanukkah, Halloween, graduation, Groundhog Day, Thanksgiving, Valentine's Day, and July 4th. Can you find the holiday symbols hidden in the picture? There are 15 all together.

(answer on page 94)

HOW DO I DO THIS RIGHT?

Take a look at some of these common problems that kids have to deal with. Try to write some of your own ideas about solving each one. You might want to ask a parent, grandparent, brother, or sister for their ideas as well.

Stop missing the bus.

_____
_____
_____

Remember my house key.

_____
_____
_____

Save money.

_____
_____
_____

Make a basket.

_____
_____
_____

FAMILY SUPPORT

The list of words below represents ideas that help create a good family life. See if you can locate them in the word search puzzle.

ACCEPT	BELIEVE	COMMUNICATE	DISCUSS
ENCOURAGE	FORGIVE	HELPFUL	HONESTY
HUG	INTEREST	KIND	KISS
LOVE	MANNERS	NICE	PLAY
PRAISE	QUESTION	RELAX	SUPPORT
TRUST	UNDERSTAND	VOLUNTEER	YIELD

```
B  P  L  A  Y  H  O  N  E  S  T  Y  O  Y  I
Y  R  V  O  L  U  N  T  E  E  R  R  I  B  W
U  A  Q  G  V  G  N  O  I  T  S  E  U  Q  S
N  I  C  E  S  E  V  X  G  S  L  L  P  S  X
D  S  I  S  S  U  C  S  I  D  C  A  H  U  T
E  E  U  O  D  A  F  K  I  N  D  X  V  P  D
R  N  R  K  W  I  R  Z  N  A  C  C  E  P  T
S  G  C  O  M  M  U  N  I  C  A  T  E  O  T
T  J  U  O  X  A  N  E  M  A  N  N  E  R  S
A  M  P  H  U  O  M  M  F  F  R  R  M  T  E
N  F  K  F  O  R  G  I  V  E  Q  Q  T  N  R
D  V  K  S  F  I  A  P  B  E  L  I  E  V  E
I  I  S  P  D  O  D  G  Y  L  R  U  D  T  T
U  P  N  L  G  X  Y  H  E  L  P  F  U  L  N
Y  J  X  F  W  W  S  S  O  H  I  V  X  M  I
```

(answer on page 94)

A MESSAGE FROM MARTY

For many years, Marty Berger, a high school student in Rockville, Maryland, served as a junior editor for *BRAKES*, providing good ideas from a kid's point of view. Marty has worked hard during this time and has been a successful student for the entire time we have known him.

Here is some advice from Marty to you:

If you have ADD (like me), there are certain things that you should do to make your life easier:

Stick to a routine.
This will help you learn discipline, and will help avoid time crunches.

Always write things down.
This way, if you forget you still have the information you will need.

Always think carefully about what you are going to do.
This, I think, is the most important factor in dealing with ADD. If you think, you will find things going your way much more often. The most important thing about living with ADD is to consider everything you do before you do it. Try to think of every possible outcome of the things you say or do. By doing that, you will avert most disasters and have many accomplishments. It takes practice, effort, and resilience. If you can stick with it, no matter when, where, or what the situation, you will be successful!

RESOURCES

BOOKS ABOUT ADD

FOR YOUNGER CHILDREN (4-8 YEARS)

Galvin, Matthew.
Otto Learns About His Medicine.
Washington, DC: Magination Press, 1988. (800-374-2721)

Moss, Deborah.
Shelly, the Hyperactive Turtle.
Bethesda, MD: Woodbine House, 1989. (800-843-7323)

Nemiroff, Marc, and Jane Annunziata.
Help Is on the Way: A Child's Book About ADD.
Washington, DC: Magination Press, 1998. (800-374-2721)

Roberts, Barbara.
Phoebe Flower's Adventures: Phoebe's Lost Treasure.
Bethesda, MD: Advantage Books, 1999. (888-238-8588)

Roberts, Barbara.
Phoebe Flower's Adventures: That's What Kids Are For.
Bethesda, MD: Advantage Books, 1998. (888-238-8588)

Sternberg, Kate.
Mama's Morning.
Bethesda, MD: Advantage Books, 1998. (888-238-8588)

FOR BOYS AND GIRLS (6-12 YEARS)

Caffrey, Jaye.
First Star I See.
Fairport, NY: Verbal Images Press, 1997.

Carpenter, Phyllis, and Marti Ford.
Sparky's Excellent Misadventures: My ADD Journal, By Me (Sparky).
Washington, DC: Magination Press, 2000. (800-374-2721)

Gehret, Jeanne.
Eagle Eyes: A Child's Guide to Paying Attention (revised ed.).
Fairport, NY: Verbal Images Press, 1991.

Gordon, Michael.
Jumpin' Johnny Get Back to Work.
DeWit, NY: GSI Publications, 1991. (315-446-4849)

Ingersoll, Barbara.
Distant Drums, Different Drummers: A Guide for Young People With ADHD.
Cape Publications, 1995.

Nadeau, Kathleen, and Ellen Dixon.
Learning to Slow Down and Pay Attention (2nd ed.).
Washington, DC: Magination Press, 1997. (800-374-2721)

Quinn, Patricia, and Judith Stern.
Putting on the Brakes: Young People's Guide to Understanding Attention Deficit Hyperactivity Disorder (ADHD).
Washington, DC: Magination Press, 1991. (800-374-2721)

Quinn, Patricia, and Judith Stern.
The "Putting on the Brakes" Activity Book for Young People With ADHD.
Washington, DC: Magination Press, 1993. (800-374-2721)

FOR TEENS

Levine, Melvin.
Keeping A Head in School.
Cambridge, MA: Educators Publishing Service, 1990.
(800-435-7728)

Nadeau, Kathleen.
Help4ADD@HighSchool.
Bethesda, MD: Advantage Books, 1999. (888-238-8588)

Nadeau, Kathleen, Ellen Dixon, and Susan Biggs.
School Strategies for ADD Teens.
Bethesda, MD: Advantage Books, 1993. (888-238-8588)

Parker, Roberta.
Making the Grade: An Adolescent's Struggle With ADD.
Plantation, FL: A.D.D. Warehouse, 1992. (800-233-9273)

Quinn, Patricia.
Adolescents and ADD: Gaining the Advantage.
Washington, DC: Magination Press, 1995. (800-374-2721)

FEELING GOOD ABOUT YOURSELF

BOOKS

Cain, Barbara.
Double Dip Feelings: Stories to Help Children Understand Emotions.
Washington, DC: Magination Press, 1991. (800-374-2721).
For ages 4-8.

Espeland, Pamela, and Rosemary Wallner.
Making the Most of Today: Daily Readings for Young People on
Self-Awareness, Creativity, and Self-Esteem.
Minneapolis, MN: Free Spirit Publishing, 1991. (800-735-7323)

Kaufman, Gershen, Lev Rafael, and Pamela Espeland.
Stick Up for Yourself: Every Kid's Guide to Personal Power and
Positive Self-Esteem (2nd revised ed.).
Minneapolis, MN: Free Spirit Publishing, 1999. (800-735-7323)

Leghorn, Lindsey.
Proud of Our Feelings.
Washington, DC: Magination Press, 1995. (800-374-2721).
For ages 3-8.

Schwartz, Linda.
A Do-It-Yourself Yearbook.
Santa Barbara, CA: The Learning Works, 1998. (800-235-5767)

GAMES

Center for Applied Psychology.
The Stop, Relax, and Think Game.
King of Prussia, PA: Childswork/Childsplay. (800-962-1141).
For ages 7-12.

GETTING ORGANIZED AT HOME AND SCHOOL

BOOKS

Cummings, Rhonda, and Gary Fisher.
The School Survival Guide for Kids With Learning Differences.
Minneapolis, MN: Free Spirit Publishing, 1991. (800-735-7323)

James, Elizabeth, and Carol Barkin.
How to Be School Smart: Super Study Skills.
New York: Beech Tree Books, 1998.

Romain, Trevor.
How to Do Homework Without Throwing Up.
Minneapolis, MN: Free Spirit Publishing, 1997. (800-735-7323)

Stern, Judith, and Uzi Ben-Ami.
Many Ways to Learn: Young People's Guide to Learning Disabilities.
Washington, DC: Magination Press, 1996. (800-374-2721).
Also available on audiotape.

BOARD GAMES

Following Directions (Red Level).
Baltimore, MD: Learning Well. (800-645-6564). For grades 2-3.

Following Directions (Blue Level).
Baltimore, MD: Learning Well. (800-645-6564). For grades 3-5.

ORGANIZATIONAL MATERIALS

"Organizational Tools for Students in Grades 3-12." Catalog available from Success by Design, 3741 Linden Ave., Wyoming, MI 49548 (800-327-0057). This catalog of useful materials for students contains items such as structured assignment notebooks and calendars.

ANSWERS

What Are the Secret Words? (page 13)
The secret message is: KEEP AT IT

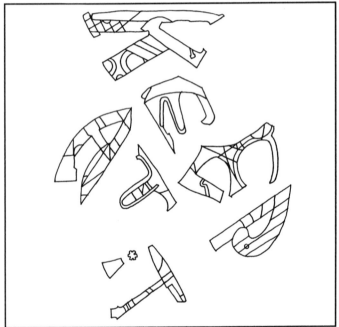

Getting Better Organized (page 15)

What is on Amy's list but is not in the picture?
Eyeglasses

What is in the picture but is not on Amy's list?
Whistle
Eraser
Backpack
Empty eyeglasses case

What did Amy forget to do?
She forgot to tie her shoelaces, and she forgot to
remove the price tag from her sweater.

Backpack Match Game (page 26)
Alex and Sam picked B and F.

What's Different? (page 28)

Tools for School (page 29)

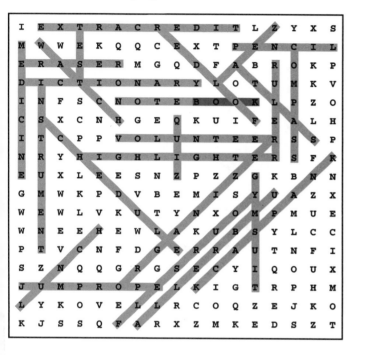

How Many Summer Fun Words Can You Find? (page 34)

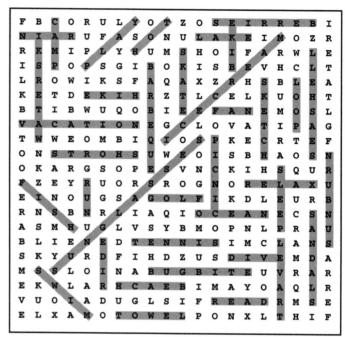

Pop Quiz (page 31)

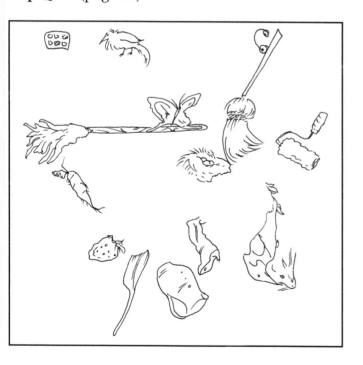

Going Camping (page 37)

Visit Mt. Fun Lodge (page 38)

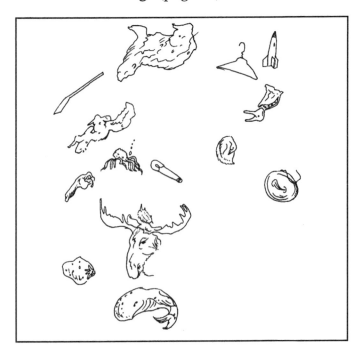

Camping Quest (page 42)

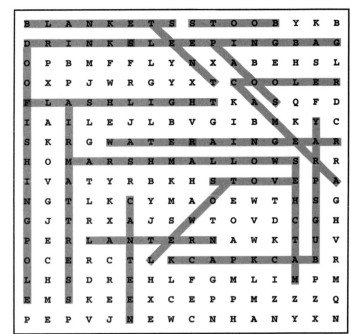

Books Crossword Puzzle (page 39)

ACROSS
1. Wilbur
3. Contents
5. Beezus
6. Stine
8. Hardy
10. Wardrobe
13. Christopher
15. Peach
17. Women
18. Index
19. Fables
20. Auto
21. Fiction

DOWN
1. Worms
2. Brown
3. Cleary
4. Science
7. Tea
8. Blume
9. Hobbit
10. Wayside
11. Dictionary
12. Cover
14. Yellow
16. Crichton

Good Sports (page 49)

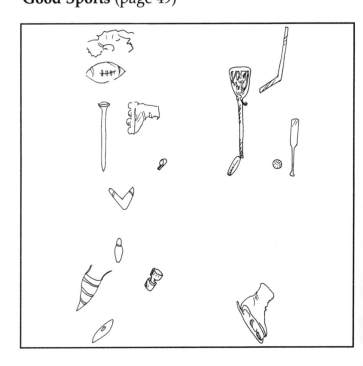

Sports Crossword Puzzle (page 51)

ACROSS
1. Hockey
4. Scuba
5. Skating
8. Diver
10. Ice
11. Soccer
12. Bowling
14. Riding
15. Yell
16. Gymnastics
17. Ball
20. Ping Pong
24. Green
25. Olympics
26. Foot

DOWN
2. Karate
3. Tennis
5. Base
6. Swimming
7. Volley
9. Running
12. Boxing
13. Golf
17. Skiing
19. Luge
21. Pool
22. Gym
23. Basket
26. Into

Super Word Search (page 65)

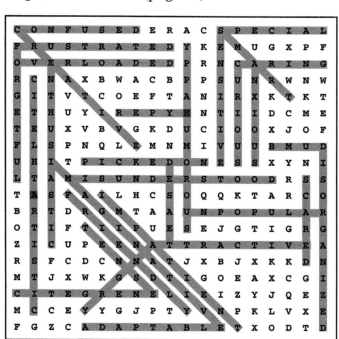

Faces and Feelings (page 62)

1G
2C
3F
4E
5A
6B
7D
8H

Find the Relatives (page 78)

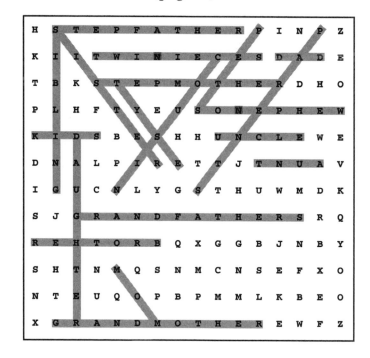

A Family Celebrates Special Times Together
(page 80)

Wedding—wedding bells
Birthday—birthday cupcake, gift
Christmas—Christmas tree, gift
Easter—Easter egg
Hanukkah—menorah, dreidel, gift
Halloween—ghost, jack-o-lantern
Graduation—graduation cap, gift
Groundhog Day—groundhog
Thanksgiving—turkey
Valentine's Day—heart (valentine)
Fourth of July—hot dog, flag

Family Support (page 82)

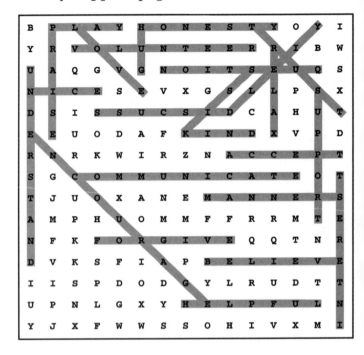